So You Want To Be Married?

Well Don't Do These Things A-Z

ANDRE L. TORRANCE

authorHOUSE®

AuthorHouse™
1663 Liberty Drive, Suite 200
Bloomington, IN 47403
www.authorhouse.com
Phone: 1-800-839-8640

First published by AuthorHouse 1/10/2009

ISBN: 978-1-4389-4016-8 (sc)

Printed in the United States of America
Bloomington, Indiana

This book is printed on acid-free paper.

Contents

Acknowledgments

I ACKNOWLEDGE EVERYONE THAT SUPPORTED me throughout this work. Your prayers and support are greatly appreciated. I would like to thank all the married couples that gave knowledge and criticisms. Your help was a great motivation to finish this project. Additionally, thank you to all my faithful readers who inspire me to continue what I do.

Message From The Author

I HOPE THIS BOOK WILL give those aspiring to be married a little insight and knowledge on what not to do in a marriage. Please note that I am not a licensed psychologist. My experience however, weighs high because of ten plus years married. I have also made some of the same mistakes. The fact of the matter is, many marriages end in divorce so any information to prevent that result could help couples. Hopefully, you will take something from this work and apply it to your relationship. Remember, no marriage is perfect and effort is required of both individuals. Stay focused on each other and keep the fire alive!!!

Good luck,
Andre L.Torrance

Get Started With A Clear Open Mind

YOU ARE ABOUT TO EMBARK on ideas and facts that you may have never thought about! Let your mind be free of any distractions. Be open for change and take whatever you can from what you are about to read for the betterment of yourself and your marriage. With that being said, take a deep breath and turn the page!!!

Allow In-Laws
To Smother New Marriage

THIS SITUATION IS GOING TO be a hard but fair one to manage. To begin, you and your mate have to be on the same page. Both of you have to be willing to accept each others in-laws and their many facets of whom they are. A measure of patience has to be made from day one, and both of you have to make a game plan for respectable space. Most in-laws are going to be very happy for the marriage and ready to spend as much time as possible getting to know the new addition to the family. The problem occurs when one and or both newlyweds feel they are obligated to entertain the parents whenever they request visiting. Parents have a way of being pushy and sometimes don't realize their excitement for a new relationship can be perceived as being nosey or needy. It's ok to have them around for special occasions but make sure you set limits and establish a force field around your new marriage. This will eliminate unwanted in-law pop-ups and confirm that you and your spouse are one. Parents are aware that the newness of a marriage can be somewhat confusing to a fresh couple; so they feel compelled to "add their two cents" in on everything they possibly can to affirm their own idealizations. You should take in all the advice given but only use the good and throw away the bad. For example, John was married for a few months and before he knew it, his mother in law was sleeping in his guest room on the night before Christmas. This situation sounds innocent, but John really expected to spend his first Christmas with his wife alone. He had so many plans of being Naked Santa, with his wife playing Mrs. Naughty Claus. That plan went to the toilet once he realized his mother desperately wanted to visit for the holidays. His first thoughts were "Hell No", but he did not want to hurt his wife's feelings because she was comfortable with it. If John disagreed to his mother in-law's visit, this would have made him look like the bad son in-law off the bat; so he agreed. In the back of John's mind he was thinking, "what have I got myself into?" I know this woman knows we just got married and are in need of new special moments with each other. Not to mention, what the hell is my wife thinking by even entertaining something like this so early in the marriage"? That simple situation caused years of anguish between John and his spouse because he always had to deal with his mother in-laws showing up on his doorstep every holiday. It created an environment of being phony just to save face. Not to mention the mother in- law did not care because she was a needy parent anyway. Situations like this caused a break down in the relationship and resulted in John feeling that his wife did not know when to say no to her mother. That's a bad way to start a relationship. Newlyweds have to realize they are the most important thing and their happiness comes from each other. They have to learn how to say no to in-laws and keep them as far away until the marriage has strength and focus. Once this is established, the newlyweds can allow in-laws in slowly with a precautionary mindset. This may seem like harsh actions towards in-laws, but it's the only way you can establish respect early in your marriage.

Battle Verbally, Physically Or Mentally

BOTH INDIVIDUALS REALLY HAVE TO work hard at this one. There are so many situations in a marriage that will cause one if not both, to be angry. The best advice is to have patience. Eliminating verbal battles is key. Time and time again when you're married, you won't see eye to eye with your spouse in many situations. This can cause one to raise their voice simply to get a point across. No harm is intended but the escalation of verbal battling is a catalyst for mental anguish. This will cause the other spouse to internalize the issue, resulting in anxiety that can affect decision making, and emotional stability in the marriage. For example, Richard came home hungry after a hard days work. His spouse was already home but had not made any attempt to prepare something for him to eat. This caused Richard to raise his voice, while simultaneously having the discussion of why his wife didn't cook. His reasoning may have been viable, but his wife took offense to his behavior and didn't want to discuss the situation due to Richard's delivery. It was perceived by his wife as aggression versus discussion with the possibility of physical abuse, which is highly unadvisable!!! The result of violent behavior can lead to incarceration depending on the woman. It can also result into bodily harm, or the marriage ending. The best way to handling any type of disagreement is by talking it out calmly, rationally and taking cool down periods. This will enable peaceful conversation and stimulate communicational growth for husband and wife without unwanted drama. Couples have to realize that neither has all the answers, but together they can conquer any issue with understanding.

Collaborate
The Tit For Tat Game

THE TIT FOR TAT GAME is a game many people have played throughout relationships. This game is not healthy nor is it at any time advisable. When one spouse does something wrong, the other can intentionally do something to hurt the spouse. All that is being done is the tit for tat game because one felt hurt from the situation. Learn that mistakes or errors happen in marriage. Be aware that neither person comes from the heavens with a halo of no wrong doing. Understand that mishaps are human nature, so move on. Don't take simple errors of your spouse to another level by having the wrong reaction. For example, Sharon came home from work late because she went with friends after work for cocktails. Sharon's husband was upset because she did not call and inform him of her decision. This resulted in Sharon's husband choosing to stay out all night with his fraternity brothers when the opportunity arose. The situation overall was cause to reaction. It sounds rather childish, but its results were descention to the marriage. Sharon felt her husband only did the tit for tat move because she had made a mistake by not calling. Now they both have frequent arguments over being considerate. The best way they should have handled this situation is by expressing unhappiness up front. All Sharon's husband had to do was express he was displeased with her actions. This would have conveyed to her that he expected her to make a more conscious effort in being considerate, which would defuse no one feeling a need for payback. When married, both individuals have to understand mistakes will be made. The good thing is that they don't have to be repeated. What needs to be done is use nuturing techniques for the relationship, and avoid doing something wrong on purpose to get back at your spouse for mistakes they have made.

Demoralize Your Marriage
For Previous Friendships
To Sustain

THE PROCESS OF FRIENDSHIP TAKES nourishing. This nourishment can be quite relative to how a new marriage also requires the same. Unknowingly, one can value previous friendships and not realize once married, some aspects should change. When married, your relationships with friends should change slightly. You have to set boundaries and guidelines. These boundaries must be adhered to because if a new marriage doesn't establish them problems will occur. Demoralization is usually one outcome because friends like in-laws, still want closeness. For example, Doug owned his home before he got married. He also had a roommate that he had known for years. Once married, his roommate moved out but always came by to visit. This visiting and various women he had accompanying him, made Doug's wife feel uneasy. The roommate also disrespected the home by frequently going in the refrigerator without asking which made the wife feel her home was being disrespected. Doug's wife also felt alienated in her own space because her husband didn't advise his friend that his behavior was not welcomed. The best way to handle situations like Doug's is to communicate with all friends. Let them know that boundaries have to be set, and that both spouses expect it. Set limits to visiting and make friends aware that visits should be given prior notice. This will stop all unwelcome visits and keep everyone on the same page. Remember, true friends understand change. They know friendships in relation to marriage takes a back seat. But if they don't know, make them aware and be stern!!!

Evolve Without Your Mate

WELL TO BEGIN, ELEVATION IN a marriage is very important. When I say elevation, I mean the act of making the marriage better. Changing throughout a marriage can have many positives. Growing and evolving can create a foundation of success and happiness. It will also increase feelings of love and compassion which all marriages need to maintain. However, many times one spouse can grow without the same equal growth of the counterpart. When I say this I mean leaving behind the other in certain aspects. For instance, Joseph and his wife Kathy both lacked college educations. Joseph realized the importance before Kathy, so he went back to school and finished his degree. Kathy on the other hand was a little different. She actually was the type of woman that needed a bigger push when it came to college so she never persued going back to school though she wanted too. Joseph's drive and determination, created success and a different outlook on life. This caused Kathy to feel that her husband was advancing in life without her and resulted in resentment. Joseph couldn't understand that his success bread jealously, envy and disparaging emotions within Kathy. He thought that his achievement would help increase household income so they could do more things, but Kathy just got mad. Married couples have to remember that both need to take steps to help each other to achieve goals. Joseph should have created a support system for Kathy, and made positive ways to help her achieve completing school also. She would have appreciated that extra push by her spouse and been happy to attend school with him as a helpmate. This would have increased a oneness in the relationship and made the household feel as if it were on the same path of success. No spouse likes to feel that they are being left behind in a marriage. Neither wants to have the thought that one is evolving more than the other. My advice would be to concentrate on goals together, and enable each other to successfully achieve dreams with a oneness of love and ambition.

Frustrate Each Other By Refusing Sex

THIS ISSUE IS TRULY ALL about who has the power. The power of seduction, which can be possessed by the man or the woman. Commonly it is the woman that has the zen that controls the sexual manifest in the relationship, and she can use it to her advantage. But to keep everything on an even playing field, we'll say both individuals involved in a marriage need to avoid using there sexual power to frustrate each other. Think of it as a game of cards. If you know you have a good hand and that you could end the game at anytime, you may choose to continue playing to past the time knowing that you have already won. Now use that same formula in reference to sex in a marriage. A spouse may know their counterpart is interested in intercourse but could delay the act until they felt like it. That action in most cases could result in frustration for the other to deal with. It can create a feeling of neglect and sexual disparity. Try to refrain from saying no as much as you say yes; meaning both individuals should take pride in the fact that they are sexual beings. Both need to be satisfied sexually. Intimacy in marriage is a key element to a happy functional relationship. Take steps to know what your spouse likes, and make a conscious effort to do it. Remember also that sex supports healthy environments in a marriage. It also will eliminate any feelings to complain of being sexually frustrated.

Gamble The Finances Away On Personal Desires

We all at one time have been rather careless with money. We have made decisions in spending based on desires and wants versus needs. A marriage from day one can have financial woes without warning. Just think, a wedding can cost up to thirty thousand dollars just on a small budget. That's not counting the wedding rings or the honeymoon. Couples in many cases are walking into financial debt straight from the alter. Debt created from one day of bells and whistles. Don't take this statement the wrong way. A proper wedding is important. It should fit the taste of the parties involved. However, if you can save money in the beginning, that could be the nest egg needed for future money woes. Take for example, a small percentage of budgeted weddings could enable a new couple to buy a home versus buying alcohol for the guests. Instead of having an open bar, do a champagne toast and keep the three thousand saved as opposed to buying liquor. Any method that you can use to cut cost in your finances do it. Don't gamble your finances away on things you won't see future results from. Big purchases should always be strategically planned. You should try to keep a method of accounting, and practice saving at least ten percent of your monthly income. This will increase the value of your savings and enable the marriage to be prepared for all those unexpected surprises.

Harbor Anger For Long Periods Of Time

WHEN PEOPLE BECOME ANGRY, IT'S usually because someone or something has influenced it. The situations can vary, but it's a human emotion to have anger. One can express it verbally, physically and emotionally. When married it is not advisable to harbor anger for long periods of time; doing that will only make the relationship worse. For example, Jay had a strong marriage for almost a year even though he was a newlywed. He and his wife got along fine. They never argued or even had disagreements until his birthday. Jay wanted to spend the first half of it with his wife, and the last portion with his buddies. At first, Jay's wife had no problem with his plans, but she later changed her mind about his plans. She let the day go by and allowed her feelings to fester internally. Her anger was then misdirected toward Jay in a later situation months after his birthday had long passed by. Jay could not understand his wife's fierce demeanor for the current disagreement. He was unaware that his wife's reasoning was beyond the current. Once the truth about the situation came out, Jay felt his wife should have spoke up on the problem during his birthday versus keeping her feelings bottled up. Married couples have to realize problems like this can occur, but can be prevented. No individual will always see eye to eye on every situation, but one must be able to communicate without being harsh. If the proper effort is put forth when dealing with harboring anger, the marriage will have a form of immunity. Remember, marriages need to have the type of communication that when one spouse stands firm on a situation, the other has to respect it. This does not mean that a spouse should behave like a tyrant. It means you should stand your ground and be able to bend to accomplish happiness for both of you. Just remember, no one wants to be with someone that's always angry.

Investigate Every Move Your Mate Makes

WHEN YOU TRUST SOMEONE, a conscious effort is made in understanding them. You can almost predict what they will and won't do. A clear understanding of who they are makes it easy and could enable you to almost put money on their quirks and attitudes. When trusted, one realizes they are trusted unconditionally without limits. Worrying about small things aren't an issue and in many cases a persons every move seems to be unimportant and unnatural. Usually, most problems of distrust do not exist until the trust is broken. This will cause the mindset to change and problems to arise. For example, when a spouse does not trust their mate, it results in disaster. The disaster could be a lifetime of unhappiness for both individuals. Good advice would be to reframe from investigating your spouses every move, unless it is warranted. Let's say your spouse doesn't trust you. The reason could be infidelity or even a questionable speaking of the truth. These issues will not change unless some form of counseling is executed, or a great evolving takes place. Many women have said that if their boyfriends cheat on them before marriage, it is inevitable that they will cheat again. This awareness is good, but it also is bad. Unknowingly, women have found that they can sometimes harbor those distrusting factors and carry them from relationship to relationship. This causes the new individual to be treated unfairly because he is paying for another person's cheating behavior. That means he will be checked up on for no reason, investigated by spouse without probable cause, and made to feel distrust issues exist. The results of these actions by an investigative spouse could damage the fabric of the marriage causing one to be sneaky and in some cases, less caring because they may feel they're never trusted anyway. The best advice in handling matters such as this is to be realistic. Don't engage yourself in any actions that would cause you to feel violated if someone did them to you. Also, make conscious efforts if the trust has been broken. Learn to accept making a mistake. It doesn't mean that your spouse doesn't love and care about you. People are human, they make dumb decisions sometime. Allow the spouse to regain that trust if it's possible. You both have to want the relationship to work. You both have to put forth effort if it means counseling, going to church for spiritual guidance or even seeking a couple's advice that has traveled down that road. Just remember, investigating a spouse's every move is not a good reaction to handling a problem that has solutions.

Jeopardize The Marriage
Being Stubborn

AN OLDER GENTLEMAN ONCE TOLD me that his wife said he was as stubborn as a mule for twenty years of their marriage. I asked him what would make a wife of twenty years make remarks like that? He advised that he never learned proper communication skills for relationships. He also said, that he was raised by his father, with no mother in the household which caused him to acquire traits of watching his father be very stern. He said that his father never faltered from decisions even if he was wrong. He also advised that growing up with that type of disfunction made it hard to communicate. He realized that the lack of compassion by a mother figure caused his adolescent childhood to be one that made him very harsh versus gentle. This negative reaction made it hard for him as an adult. The older gentleman stated that he realized his inability to communicate effectively without being mean was a big problem. In fact, it trickled into every relationship he ever had and his marriage of twenty years. He said it was always a constant battle to be mindful of what came out of his mouth. Many situations resulted in fierce arguments because he wasn't willing to bend. Various nights on the couch was a frequent in his household because his wife was angry with him for talking to her so abruptly. Overall, he had a long difficult marriage. He admitted that he could have changed his ideologies a long time ago, but never explained to his wife why he behaved like he did. He realized that if he had taken that extra step, his wife could have helped him with his problem versus being the receiver of his issues. The situation of being stubborn can have many affects on a marriage. It can cause fierce arguments, a disliking of your spouse and a unhappy marriage for years. Spouses must realize that being stubborn doesn't help the situation, and it will block blessings and leave scars that never heal. Remember one can change if the desire is there.

Keeping Secrets Of The Past

We all have heard the expression "I will take something I'm not proud of to my grave". Though the implied meaning is a strong statement, it enables one to keep secrets. When married, one should not participate in activities such as this. Not talking about key situations that may have happened in the past, can destroy a marriage. For example, Ray was a model college student. He never missed class and made good grades throughout his college years. The only problem was that Ray used marijuana frequently to help alleviate study anxiety. His girlfriend was aware that he smoked but didn't see his frequent use. Ray later married his college girlfriend but still smoked marijuana heavily. The only difference was that his body became ammune to it and it didn't affect him the same as it once did in college. He began experimenting with cocaine to get a new high. This act was unknowing to his wife and went on for years. It did not come to light until Ray was stopped by the police for speeding while on vacation with his family. His wife and two daughters were all shocked when the policeman found cocaine in the car. Ray was placed under arrest in front of his wife and kids and taken to jail. His wife didn't understand how he was using cocaine for so many years and she was never aware. Ray told her that he knew he needed help with the drug use problem, but felt it was easier to keep it a secret handling it on his own. The family is now facing various issues because the bread winner of the family is behind bars with hefty fines. Keeping secrets from your spouse is not a good idea. It can leave damaging effects just like Ray and his family. The ramifications can create situations leaving a family in turmoil and disparity. It can also tarnish the relationship beyond repair. Keeping secrets of the past is selfish behavior. It hurts the family, and should never be a choice when dealing with the ones that matter in your life.

Lie About The Truth

BEING TRUTHFUL IS A TRAIT that is learned not taught. To have truth is divine because it enables one to be honest. This honesty is taken throughout life in many situations. Many have learned that telling the truth has many effects. It can sometimes enable one's well being, or even crush ones self esteem. When in marriage though, It's better to tell the truth to your spouse than to lie. If you are not fond of your spouse's cooking, it's better to say so than go for years not mentioning it. If your not happy with your husband's bad eating habits which resulted in weight gain tell him. When married you must be able to express yourself and let the other know what you like and don't care for. This does not mean belittle your spouse but rather don't lie. I've been told that one grows thick skin when married. You learn to be critical and in some cases overbearing. You learn to be understanding not knowing this can create an environment where the truth is sometimes placed on the back burner because of feelings. As a result, marriages become an environment were the truth is told only if it doesn't affect the relationship. A spouse doesn't say to the other; "I'm not fond of your father" or "I think your brother is a moocher". Instead we keep it bottled up inside and try to avoid the root of our disliking. We may tell a close friend about our feelings, but we tend not to discuss these sensitive matters with our spouse. This act just creates an environment for lying and not being forthcoming with the truth. It also enables a sense of animosity in the dislikes, and could make one feel they are forced to deal with situations because they have no choice. When married, you should learn to put your spouse before you, but frequently discuss your personal feelings. This will stop you from having a toxic mindset when dealing with touchy issues. You don't have to avoid the truth by lying to your spouse. Any situation deserves a line of communication. This enables your relationship to be without blocked truths being told, and stops frequent drama within the marriage from lies.

Manipulate The Marriage
For A Selfish Opportunity

THE WORD MANIPULATE IS DEFINED as a way of using control to manage or influence a situation by being devious. This definition can be used in many ways to explain why manipulation is a shrewd way of handling issues. Marriages can be manipulated also, and should be addressed. Throughout the course of any marriage, one spouse usually has more influence than the other. There is not a specific reasoning for this, it just happens. Most of the time, the other spouse involved doesn't know why it's like that but accepts it. This in most cases can destroy the fabric of the relationship. That's why I believe manipulation in a marriage for selfish reasons or opportunity is something couples shouldn't do. For example, James and his wife always had a pretty good relationship. James actually praised his wife for her beauty on a regular basis. He always brought her new clothes and kept her hair and nails done monthly. James was always rewarded for his kind gestures with more hugs and kisses than he could sometimes handle. The only problem was that James' wife was very shy around others. One day James was approached by a friend at work that had an associate who was in the modeling industry. He noticed a picture of James' wife on his desk while walking through the office. The guy was very interested in shooting some pictures of James' wife for a story on attractive married women. James was very excited about the idea, but was well aware that his wife would say no because of her shyness. James made up a story and told his wife that his boss requested the favor of his wife to take the pictures, almost making it seem like he would loose his job if she didn't. James' wife felt compelled to do it because of the situation. She was aware that it would be a tough experience for her due to her timidity, but she went through with the photo shoot anyway. She also never found out the truth about why she was chosen to take the photos in the first place because they were scrapped in the final layout. The only one that knew the truth was James. Actually to this day, he never told his wife the truth about his manipulative act. Surely if she was aware, she would be furious about how he handled the situation. This example sounds simple in nature, but could have major results if the truth were exposed. This is why spouses should never manipulate each other for selfish opportunities. It's wrong and does not have a place in a marriage that is supposed to be loving and caring. Couples should always be honest about situations no matter what; even if they think their spouse would disagree with it. It is better to lay all your cards on the table than to manipulate someone you're suppose to love by being deceitful.

Negotiate Your Marriage With Anyone But Your Spouse

NEGOTIATION IS A KEY ELEMENT in the survival of any marriage. The problem with negotiation is when spouses do it outside the marriage. This can create problems within it. For instance, if you think your spouse is a workaholic; you shouldn't rely on your friends to keep you company especially if they are all single. That atmosphere can make you behave unknowingly like your single. You can become complacent about your spouses needs and even begin to be less caring about their emotions. These acts are not intentional, but are the results of the singles way of thinking. Meaning, you care about yourself because you only have to worry about yourself. Single individuals sometimes unknowingly treat married friends like they are still single. They feel compelled to keep the friendship going on the same path that it was on before the friend got married. This act can sometimes have grave consequences on a marriage because the spouse may feel he or she isn't number one in the other person's life. It may sound far fetched, but you would be surprised how many married couples have this problem throughout their relationship. One way to find out if your friends really care about you being married, is to count how many times they ask how you're doing versus how is your marriage going? If you realize they ask more about your wellbeing in comparison to the marriage you're in, a light should go off in your head illustrating there is a possible lack of respect. Don't be offended by this situation, just explain to your friends that your marriage is number one in your life. Also, make them aware that their behavior should be respectful to the fact you are married but still able to sustain friendships with the proper understanding of all involved. If you do these things, your friendship will stay wholesome and your marriage will stand the test of time. Always avoid negotiating your marriage with friends over your spouse.

Overwhelm Each Other With Small Issues

Experienced married people handle situations differently than single people. They try to conquer problems fast and usually with care. The reason is because they don't like for problems to fester and become overwhelming. Regardless if it's something that can be handled individually or with both parties, they attack it knowing something has to be done. This mindset helps to prevent disaster when unnecessary issues arise and limits them from becoming bigger ones. For example, issues like who cooked last or even deciding what television program to watch can have many effects on a marriage. They can basically cause happiness or grief. Actually, they can make the marriage worse because small issues like that have been known to overwhelm marriages when bigger issues are already stressful. Married people have to understand that if you and your spouse both work, it should never be an issue of who's preparing dinner. If it takes both of you combining skills to make a meal, just do it. This will enable more quality time for enjoying each other's company versus creating an environment for anxiety. Couples should also make self-internalizations over small issues to establish if they are even worth bothering the other spouse. Independent mindsets help to elevate unnecessary involvement. I believe most spouses would love for a small issue to be taken care of by the counterpart because it shows drive and self-empowerment. Statistics have shown that most husbands don't worry about their wife regularly making bad choices if they have good decision skills. I also know that many wives have said they respect their husbands more when they know he will take charge of some issues to alleviate problems. This in some cases, can stop impact to the family positively or negatively.

Overall, the plan in any marriage should be a team effort. Both individuals must strive to keep the marriage running smoothly and avoid overwhelming each other with small issues that can be handled individually. This act will alleviate wasted time and keep a sense of motivation in the marriage.

Procrastinate Getting Counseling With Spouse

IN THE GAME OF BASKETBALL you have two teams. They play against each other to score points and show who has the most skill. A referee monitors the game. This individual is usually very knowledgeable about playing the game. He decides if players on either team break rules, and gives slight advice to prevent players from making mistakes. A counselor in some cases can be considered a referee of sorts also. The reason is because he officiates relationships. He gives married couple's a different way of looking at things and shows them how to better there relationship. Marriage counselors say, "If you feel your relationship needs help, get it"! They say this because they know many married people never really understand why they are not compatible. They also are aware that if couples don't seek out help, situations could become worse. This is the chief reason for high divorce rates in the U.S. Some married people will know they have issues, and just avoid talking about it. They procrastinate and keep making the same mistakes repeatedly. If they only tried counseling, some problems could get answers and solutions. These solutions enable one to view their spouse's feelings, and can depict a clear view from an unbiased source. They can also motivate an understanding of the spouse's behavior. Avoiding counseling makes the situation worst. It damages the fabric of the relationship, and becomes a negative for both involved. It creates self esteem issues and could make one person doubt the strength of the marriage. As the old saying goes "actions speak louder than words." Meaning, if you're not making an attempt to fix what's wrong by taking action, stop running your mouth until you're ready to do something about it!!! Seeking counseling will help most situations, but avoiding it will not. Avoidance could actually destroy the relationship. The best advice is don't procrastinate counseling. If you want your relationship to have a fighting chance, go get it!

Quarrel Over Pettiness

MOST RELATIONSHIPS WILL HAVE GOOD and bad times. They will have varying issues but similar outcomes if not handled properly. Usually, arguing over small petty situations can create non- positive environments. A way to avoid this negativity is to avoid quarrelling over the small things. For example, if your mate snores when sleeping, it would be best to try and fix the problem versus letting it fester. Allowing a snoring mate to continue for long periods could create an on going issue. Taking the time to fix the problem will keep you from having quarrels on the subject. Sure it's a small thing, but it could become a big one. Remember that most marriages fail because of small things. Spouses hold on to issues instead of addressing them initially. This holding on to marital problems just isn't healthy. It prevents nurturing through communication and eliminates open forums for discussions. Try to avoid this behavior all together. Stay positive with your feelings as much as possible. This will empower the marriage to handle any situation it faces. Rather good or bad, the outcome will be positive.

Refuse Guidance From
Viable Sources.

A WISE MAN ONCE SAID, "knowledge is power". This power in relation to marriage can be a positive or negative thing when it comes to where the knowledge is coming from. It's actually hard to believe that some married couples very seldom seek information on marriage from viable sources. They rarely ask couples that have been married for years how they did it. The thought of asking a divorced couple where they went wrong never comes to mind. Instead, married couples talk to their friends and family who in most cases, have nothing positive to bring to the table. For example, Stacey was a newlywed who didn't have many positive relationship examples in her circle. Her mother didn't have a husband, and actually kept Stacey and her younger brother from having a relationship with their father. The excuse she gave them for making that decision was never accepted by Stacey. It caused her to unknowingly have a limited respect for men. She tried to be the wife to her new husband for a couple of months; then changed. The change came when Stacey and her husband were having a discussion on a wife humbling herself to make the marriage better. This didn't sit well with Stacey and actually made her demeanor thereafter, quite stubborn. Her husband realized the change in attitude and tried to seek advice but looked in the wrong place. He went to his male friend that had been dating the same woman for the past two years. The problem was that the girlfriend was someone else's wife. That's right she was married and had been cheating on her husband more than half of the five years they were together. People like that don't qualify as the right individuals to seek marital advice from. Truth is, anyone that doesn't have a sustained positive nurturing relationship shouldn't be sought out for marriage advice. They will only give you a distorted, toxic and one sided way of thinking. The information given will more than likely be disfunctional and should be avoided at all cost. Try to indulge your marital advice from people that have a history of positive functional marriages. Choose the ones that can speak with knowledge and show clear examples of how there own relationship has worked. Avoid the people that are functioning worse than you are in a relationship. Misery loves company. Try to keep individuals out of your marriages business. Also, involve your relationship around married people. Remember, single people are single for a reason, and getting guidance from non-viable sources will only damage your marriage in the long run.

Stifle Your Mate From Whom They Are As An Individual

Derrick was married to Janice about five years. They had a good relationship for the most part but Janice always felt that Derrick stifled her from being an individual. Janice was free spirited and loved to be with people. Derrick was a home body that never did much but go to work. He actually expected his wife to stay home and never go out. This caused Janice to rebel because it was out of her character. They both realized that this problem was starting to become more of an issue. Derrick realized that his mindset could possibly be one sided, so he asked Janice to take the proper steps in not feeling that way anymore. He told her to start doing the things that she wanted to do. Janice proceeded to be free and actually felt better about her self. The feelings of Derrick were mixed because he sensed that this new found freedom was causing his marriage to fall apart. He began to mistrust his wife because she was always gone, and felt that this new found freedom was a way of her behaving like a single woman versus a married one. Derrick just didn't like the idea of presenting his feelings because this would only revert he and Janice back to moments when they initially encountered the problem. Derrick eventually had enough, and demanded that his wife do as he wished or he wanted a divorce. By then, Janice was so far gone in being her own person that she didn't even care. So to sum it up, Derrick and Janice got divorced because they didn't see eye to eye on the stifling your mate situation. (((MESASAGE)) Gather what you feel is important from this story and apply it to your situation. If you can, just remember no marriage is perfect and no matter what you do, sometimes things just don't work out.

Tempt Your Spouse
To Anger

TEMPTING YOUR SPOUSE TO ANGER can have many affects. Many marriages suffer because of this. In many cases, the relationship has irreversible issues that can never be forgotten. Regular existence of anger outbursts from one spouse to another makes staying together difficult. As humans, we experience a lot of emotions. Bursts of impulsive anger could have an unknown suppressed toleration, support, love or concern. It is important to understand why a spouse may behave in an angry manner. Progress can be made with visible success. It can result in actually making the marriage stronger if the proper steps are taken. So, I guess now is a good time to tell you how to diffuse your mate from having anger outbursts. The first thing you need to do is understand that this usually comes from discussions or disagreements. Once the situation occurs, it is best to give a cool down period. Do that before even bringing the issue up again. Do realize that if your spouse mentions the subject before you again, you may need to change your approach and try discussing it a different way. Realize that couples have a tendency of such intent to find an answer to the problem that they often fail to do the obvious which is self-examination. Be real with yourself and ask if you had a hand in igniting the anger. Ask yourself questions like, " Do I nag constantly?" Nagging is one way to cause anger outburst. There may also be other reasons too. Note that anger outbursts can result in physical and emotional abuse. So try to talk to your spouse with a caring and gentle language. Show that you have forgiven the person and are willing to get things back to normal. Once the lines of communication are better, talk to your partner about the situation getting to the bottom of the issue. This will create a positive, harmonious relationship. Identify the origins and causes of your spouses anger and pinpoint the steps to prevent it from reoccurring. If you do all these things, I believe your relationship will have hope and a change of behavior permanently.

Undermine Your Spouse

THIS SUBJECT IS IN REFERENCE to marriages that involve children. Most parents know that kids rely heavily on their parents. They need them for guidance, protection and love. One way that children can get a sense of security is by knowing they can depend on both parents to provide the necessary boundaries for their day-to-day life. An example of this would be dividing daily chores and responsibility tasks. Such actions are very important in teaching children the fundamentals of adult life. The problem however, is parents can sometimes undermine each other when it comes to this process. They inadvertently allow their children to influence decision-making, which can limit there spouse's authority. Ways resolution can be achieved is by returning certain privileges that were taken by one spouse because of behavior issues, or not backing your spouse on enforcing rules that have been broken. These offenses can leave mixed impressions on children making them understand which parent to go to for certain things. You as a parent can avoid situations like this by talking to your spouse and being on the same page when making decisions. Conversations with spouses should be ongoing discussions as children grow. Time outs and other disciplines should be agreed to and followed through. Removal of privileges for reasonable amounts of times may apply to certain ages and intelligence levels of the child. For example, if a child doesn't yet understand wetting the bed is a problem, how can you punish him or her for something not yet comprehensible? Realize that discipline is a hard decision to make, so do it with care and compassion. Children need to see that you and your spouse are a support center for them. They need to see their parents as a united front. They need to know that both parents are equally invested in the commitment to raising happy, respectful and kind human beings. Following the above small ideas will help you to achieve this gracefully. Just try to avoid undermining your spouse when it comes to the children.

Violate Your Vows Of Marriage

I wanted to express something that made a huge impact on my life. When I made my vows to my wife on July 1, 2000, I made them for my entire natural life. Those vows were during sickness and in health, richer or poorer and forsaking all others. It is the forsaking all others that I want to focus on in this chapter. I came out of a lifestyle that included some very promiscuous thinking and actions. This all changed when I became married, but the pictures and memories of my past seem burned into my mind. As I make decisions on people I associate with, places I go, and things I think I make certain to guard my mind as I venture into those areas. For me, forsaking all others is more than crossing the line and abandoning my marriage vows. It means that I strive not to allow my mind or eyes to wander from my wife. I do this for three reasons. First, my Lord is important and dear to me. I have covenanted with him that he has complete control of my life. It is not that I live for Him, but that He lives through me. I understand that this vessel can stray, but it will not stray as long as I allow Him complete control. Second, my family is precious and dear to me. I have covenanted with my wife that she is the only woman that I will ever desire. I have promised my wife that I will not do anything that will remove the stability of the family. I know that I am not the nicest person nor the best provider financially, but I will make certain that she understands stability because her husband is not going anywhere. My wife knows and depends on the fact that I am not going to place myself in any position that will cause others to question my commitment to her. Third, try to think like a grandparent married for fifty years. I try to keep myself grounded with a mature way of thinking. I avoid acting like a person that can have no consequences for there actions. Older people think before they act. They care about their spouse more than themselves. They always keep their marriage top priority over friends, functions and sometimes family. They also try at least once a day, to let their counterpart know they are loved dearly. Applying this way of thinking will not be an easy task. It takes and requires a lot of patience, understanding and willingness to bend. Remember that no one person knows everything about the relationship of marriage, but all should know that violating your vows of marriage is not pleasing to God; so don't do it.

Withdraw Yourself From Communication

THIS TOPIC IS A HELPFUL hint for women who can't understand why men withdraw themselves from communication. Many women don't understand that men are just as strange as they are. In fact, men have there odd ways of handling things and believe they are right in doing them. What women need to understand is that this behavior can be influenced by yours.

First of all, women must understand that hiding their true feelings from a man in fear that sharing your want of a closer relationship and love is smart; your right! It could scare him away. Unfortunately, everything has a time and place so don't be so eager to tell someone your true feelings until you know their actions show feelings developing towards you.

Second, now that you have your man, be mindful of how you talk to him in reference to the relationship. If you come across as being demanding, that will shut down the lines of communication quickly. Most men don't like to feel that they are being forced to act a certain way in their relationship by the mate. They will accept it easier if they feel the relationship calls for action versus you suggesting that they are the problem. Try to communicate with a passion of caring versus being demanding. Men are more prone to accept this type of communication when they feel they can help be the problem solver. Thirdly, develop a physical, emotional and social environment with your man. Take time to nurture effective communication in any situation. Men don't like to have discussions with someone they aren't closely connected with. Don't ask your man a direct question that you know may upset him. Instead, play your womanly role and get the answers to the question by treading softly around the subject. Your man will more than likely fall into that situation with better outcomes for you.

Thirdly, try not to be a nag. Nagging is one of man's biggest complaints. They don't like to be constantly questioned about everything they do. They usually feel that it is a big turn off to be constantly questioned about feelings and overwhelmed with things that aren't important to the day-to-day activities. Realize that I am not saying don't communicate but try to keep unnecessary questioning to a minimum. Make your man like talking to you about subjects versus always regretting talking. Keep the type of open line of communication, that he will enjoy. Most of the time as you learn your mate, you will know when the right time to talk is available. You will understand that communication with them has a time and place, and you will learn to think before you speak.

Talking is important in any relationship. Remember, don't discuss your feelings until the time is right. Be mindful of your delivery to him when communicating and don't be a nag. If you follow this advice, more than likely your man will never withdraw from having a positive line of communication with you.

Run From New Ideas
When It Comes To Sex

How DO YOU KEEP THINGS hot and steamy at the end of a long day? It's not always easy to find time and energy for the one you love. From jobs to kids, to household chores, the last thing on you mind is sex right? Well let me tell you what to do.

1. Communication is the key to a healthy and active sex life in a marital relationship, so talk with one another more!

2. Share with one another your sexual desires.

3. Talk with one another about your expectations concerning lovemaking. False or unmet expectations can hurt your marriage.

4. Sexual intimacy is a continuing process of discovery. True intimacy through communication is what makes sex great.

5. Sex in a long lasting relationship can deepen and become a richer experience. No matter how many times you have made love to each other, the wonder and awe of mutual attraction can still be there.

6. When life becomes busy and schedules are hectic, plan for sexual encounters with one another. Make sex one of your main priorities.

7. Try to set the mood in advance.

8. If you want to have good sex at night, start the foreplay in the morning.

9. Let your spouse know you care and are thinking about him/her throughout the day by notes, e-mails, phone calls, hugs, etc.

Following the above simple steps can and will increase your sex life. This will also make things flow in your relationship. Just remember to avoid running from new ideas, and try to always please your spouse.

Use Harsh Words
That Can't Be Taken
Back Once Said

PERSONAL ATTACKS UPON YOUR SPOUSE with harsh words, innuendoes, exaggeration, or blame is incredibly destructive to your entire relationship. The chief problem with such attacks are they fail to resolve anything with reference to the conflict itself. In fact, they usually only intensify your differences. Corrupt communication is not only swearing or foul language, but any words that tear someone down instead of building him or her up. Saying things like, "You are a slob", "I hate you," " You are so pigheaded," or "If you don't like it, why don't you divorce me?" only serve to destroy the relationship and corrupts what's left in the marriage. You need to stop this kind of language today while there is still time to repair your relationship. The worst thing about attacking your partner is the fact that you never get around to attacking the problem. Failing here, only assures you that this conflict will come up again very soon. How can you keep yourself from getting into the attack mode? One of the simplest ways is to use wisdom in your choice of words. When communicating with your spouse you might say, *"Robert, I am very frustrated with these clothes on the floor. Can we talk this over?"*, or *"Honey when I come home and have to step over toys and shoes just to get to the kitchen, it sets me off before I can even say hello. Can we talk about this?"* In addition, controlling your anger will greatly help you to refrain from personally attacking your spouse. Anger always begins to boil inside your heart when you hold on to an offense day after day without resolving it. Resolving issues quickly will keep you from those volcanic eruptions where you spew out the resentments from several previous conflicts. You must learn how to *"stop contention before a quarrel starts."* (Prov. 17:14). Controlling your anger can also be accomplished by simply asking God to fill you with his Holy Spirit. It's not enough to simply want to control your anger, you need a power beyond yourself to help you do it. Paul said if you would *"walk in the Spirit you would not fulfill the desires of the flesh"* (Gal. 5:16). It all comes down to a matter of choice when you are dealing with the issues of conflict. Do you want to resolve the issues or allow them to continue to fester? Do you want to discuss the problems in a controlled way or explode and resolve nothing? Do you want to do it God's way or try and handle it your way? It's your choice.

Making Bad Decisions You Know Will Destroy The Relationship

RELATIONSHIPS ARE OFTEN HARD TO maintain, even when two people profess undying love for each other. A major problem in a relationship is that one or both partners continue to make the same errors but then cannot understand why the relationship is in trouble. It is almost as though they are determined to do things their way, even at the risk of damaging a good thing. I have listed a few things that will destroy your relationship if you make these types of bad decisions.

1. Rigidly maintaining that you are always right, even when you do not have all the facts!

2. Never apologizing, even when you are proven wrong beyond a shadow of a doubt!

3. Being relentless in rubbing it in when you are proven right!

4. Dogmatically maintaining that you know your partner's motives better than he or she does!

5. Assuming that your partner should understand your needs and should respond immediately without being asked!

6. Totally ignoring your partner's priorities and insist on your own!

7. Operating on the assumption that your partner's sexual need cycle is identical to yours!

8. Adding deep psychological meaning to your partner's sexual disinterest and taking it very personally!

9. Not ever admitting hurt, transitioning immediately to the expression of anger!

10. Identifying your partner's character flaws and family secrets and using them to make a point when logic fails! Try to avoid doing the things that I have listed in reference to making bad decisions in your relationship. Not doing so can destroy the relationship. If you value this advice, I think your relationship will have a chance at making it.

Helpful Hints For Her

(JUGGLING IS NOT JUST FOR Clowns)-Meaning just because you have to go to work, clean the house, and take care of the kids, that does not mean you can't take time out for yourself. Manage your time wisely and you will see that everything will fall into place. Don't get frustrated and allow your feelings to fester. If you need the help of your mate, just ask for it. Don't create bigger problems by keeping things bottled up inside.

(Cooking Is Legal)- This basically refers to feeding your household properly. Many men today complain on a regular basis about the loss of the wife in the kitchen. Women must realize the old saying that "the way to a man's heart is thru his stomach", is true. There is nothing wrong with eating out sometimes due to lifestyle, but a home cooked meal made with love goes a long way with any man.

(If You Won't Someone Else Will)- Show compassion to your husband. Do the things he likes in bed. Make him feel that you are his private hooker if need be. Tell each other all your kinky fantasies to keep the spice in the marriage. Though sex is not the basis for a relationship, it is a viable facet.

(Switch Up The Night Ware)- Bloomers and sweatshirts are not sexy to most men. We do understand that sometimes women want to be comfortable in bed, but keep that type of outfit to a minimum. Wear outfits that will enhance some intimacy and keep the fire going with sexy nightgowns. Please also remember not to wear hair rollers every night; it's not sexy to most men...

(A King Loves His Queen)- Women should always know that men love to be treated like a king. This treatment can be running his bath water or rubbing his back. The job may sound hard to some women but believe and know that if you do special things for him, your reward will be double what you put in.

Helpful Hint For Him

(SLAVERY IS OVER) - THERE is nothing wrong with helping out with chores around the house. When you assist your wife in the day to day cleaning or housework, it shows that you're not a slave driver. It also illustrates your desire to be a team player in getting the jobs done so you can relax with each other.

(Trash Is Her Enemy)- Many women would prefer not to take out or deal with trash in any way. Due to this fact, make it easy on her by grabbing the trash at moments notice. Frequently keep an eye on the trash and monitor taking it out. This will make things easy around the house because anytime it gets full; she won't have to ask you to dump it.

(Good Hygiene Before Bed Is A Plus)- Women love a man that is clean and smells good. Keep your hygiene up to par before bed. This will increase the chances of more intimacy and cuddling because you smell good and are clean. Not to mention, women have a big problem with men that have obvious body odor.

(A Clean Vehicle Represents You)- An old man once told me that a way you can find out if a woman has a man is to look at the cleanliness of her car. Car maintenance should be the mans responsibility and he should make sure that his spouse's car is always clean inside and out. He should also make sure engine, brakes and tune-ups are up to par. After all you should think of your wife as precious cargo and her car should be mechanically sound, clean and safe for driving.

(She Shops You Carry)-No woman wants to spend time doing all the household shopping, load the car up then drive home with all the packages purchased. What makes the situation worse is that they really don't want to have to carry all the packages in the house by themselves while you sit in front of the television watching them do it. If your wife takes the time to go get the groceries, you should be able to help unload the car and carry them inside. You can even take it a step father by assisting in putting them up.

For Both Of You

1) Healthy relationships need chemistry to enable feelings of dual emotion especially when there is some type of attraction that exists.

2) Remain committed; which will enable the relationship to stay focused when there are highs and lows.

3) Establish trust, which will show I know you and I am aware of what you will do and won't.

4) Take responsibility for your actions no matter if they are positive or negative.

5) Exercise honesty and open lines of communication to understand each other's feelings.

6) Acknowledge compatibility to explain what you expect in the relationship to sustain it.

7) Sustain communication and the willingness to talk about any and everything that relates to achieving happiness for all that's involved.

For Both Of You

THERE IS NOTHING WRONG WITH having date nights and treating the relationship like it's new. Often times people in marriages think they can't do certain things with each other because they are married now. That is not true and should not be a common practice. Try to keep that same momentum. Don't loose what made you a couple at the start of your unity. Be respectful and stay compassionate like you was when dating. Try to maintain that awareness of each other's feelings and practice it as much as you can. Also, remember that marriage should be a fun thing not a death wish. It should be treated with care just like one does at the beginning of a relationship. Go out to your special places and snuggle up sometimes. Even sneak off away from friends to have sex if that rocks your boat. Just be spontaneous like you use to be and keep the fire going.

Take Notes

Take Notes

Take Notes

Take Notes

Take Notes

_____

_____

_____

_____

_____

_____

_____

_____

_____

_____

_____

_____

_____

_____

_____

_____

_____

_____

_____

_____

_____

Take Notes

_____

_____

_____

_____

_____

_____

_____

_____

_____

_____

_____

_____

_____

_____

_____

_____

_____

_____

_____

_____

_____

_____

_____

_____

Take Notes